Table of Contents

Fan's Dictionary – Sheffield U**r** Songbook

Over the years Sheffield United F.C. fans have created incredible atmospheres in football grounds and come up with some of the creative chants and songs. This book is a guide for these chants and songs written by the Sheffield United F.C. supporters. From Allez Allez Allez, Greasy Chip Butty, Barrel of Money, Falling in Love With You, Forever And Ever, Glory Glory Sheff United, to songs dedicated to the various players and staff, the very best of the terrace chants, songs, and timeless classics, this book will delight and entertain in equal measure and honors every single Sheffield United F.C. fan who has ever sung in support for the team throughout its proud history.

All the songs and chants in this book are written and sang by the Sheffield United F.C. supporters during football matches, at pubs and bars or posted to message boards, they are not the thoughts or views of the authors.

WRITE TO US

We greatly value your opinion. We would love to hear your thoughts and recommendations about this book so we can improve! Write to us: fansdictionary@gmail.com

COPYRIGHT

ADRIAN LITTLEJOHN

Robin Hood left Sherwood, to come to
Bramall Lane,
Pleaded with Dave Basset, please give my
boy a game,
Dave Bassett said to the man in green,
To be a Blade, you've got to play like Brian
Deane.
Robin Hood was no good, it was such a
shame,
Friar Tuck got kicked to f***, he couldn't
play the game,
All was not lost, Bassett got his man (who),
Littlejohn, Littlejohn, Littlejohn.
Littlejohn, Littlejohn running down the
wing,
Littlejohn, Littlejohn, fastest thing we've
seen,
He's black as coal, he'll score a goal,
Littlejohn, Littlejohn, Littlejohn...

ALAN BIRCHENALL

Sherman, Sherman, Sherman...

ALAN CORK

Alan Cork, Alan Cork, Alan Alan Cork,
He's got no hair, but we don't care,
Alan Alan Cork.

ALAN WOODWARD

We've got Alan Alan Alan Alan Woodward,
on the wing, on the wing,
We've got Alan Alan Alan Alan Woodward,
on the wing, on the wing,
Alan, Alan Woodward, Alan Woodward on
the wing,
Alan, Alan Woodward, Alan Woodward on
the wing.

ALLEZ ALLEZ ALLEZ

We are Sheff United,
They call us the Blades,
We got Billy Sharp,
He's a legend at the Lane,
Basham and O'Connell,
Overlapping down the wings,
Duffy, Fleck and Norwood,
With his f*cking ping,
Allez Allez Allez (x4),
Chris Wilder is our gaffer,
He leads us all the way,
Playing proper football,
The Sheffield United way,
Allez Allez Allez (x4),
He stuck the paper on the wall,
They called us journeymen,
Now we're going on a journey,
To the f*cking prem,
Allez Allez Allez (x4).

AND IT'S SHEFFIELD UNITED

And it's Sheffield United,
Sheffield United FC,
We're by far the greatest team,
The world has ever seen...

ARE YOU WEDNESDAY IN DISGUISE

Are you Wednesday,
Are you Wednesday,
Are you Wednesday in disguise,
Are you Wednesday in disguise...

ARTURO LUPOLI

Arturo Lupoli,
Arturo Lupoli,
Arturo Lupoli,
Arturo Lupoli...

BARREL OF MONEY

We ain't got a barrel of money,
We ain't got Woodward or Currie,
But with Eddie Colquhoun,
Promotion is so,
United,
All together now...

BERTIE MEE SAID TO BILL SHANKLY

Bertie Mee said to Bill Shankly,
Have you heard of the North Bank
Highbury,
He said No, I don't think so,
But I've heard of the Shoreham Aggro /
SUFC.

BERTIE MEE SAID TO BILL SHANKLY 2

Bertie Mee said to Bill Shankly,
Have you heard Alan Brown has got VD,
He said yes, he's in a mess,
And so are the Wednesday FC.

BILLY SHARP

We've got Billy Sharp, Billy Sharp,
We've got Billy Sharp,
Na na na na na na na.

BRIAN DEANE AND TONY AGANA

Brian Deane and Tony Agana,
Bibbety bobbity boo,
Put them together and what have you got?
Top of division 2.

BRIAN HOWARD

De, de, de, de, Brian Howard,
De, de, de, de, Brian Howard.

BRING ON

Bring on Man United bring on Chelsea,
Bring on the Scottish by the score,
There's the Rangers in the Blue & the Celtic
in the Green,
But we're still the finest team you've ever
seen.

BUILD A BONFIRE

Build a bonfire,
Build a bonfire,
Put the Wednesday on the top,
Dirty Leeds in the middle,
And we'll burn the f**kin lot...

CAN YOU HEAR US ON THE BOX

Sheffield Wednesday,
Sheffield Wednesday,
Can you hear us on the box,
Can you hear us on the box...

CARL ASABA

When the ball hits the goal,
It's not Shearer or Cole,
It's Asaba.

CHEAT

Cheat, Cheat, Cheat, Cheat...

CHED EVANS

Super, super Ched,
Super Chedwyn Evans.

CHED EVANS 2

We bought the lad from Man City called
Ched, called Ched,
I'll fire you to the Premier League, he said,
he said,
He scored a goal and that was it,
The Shoreham boys they had a fit,
Cheddy Evans, United's number 9.

CHED EVANS 3

He'll s*ag who he wants,
He'll s*ag who he wants,
It's our boy Cheddy Evans,
He'll s*ag who he wants...

CHED EVANS 4

He's coming home, he's coming home,
Ched Evans, Chedwyn's coming home.

CHRIS MORGAN

Number 1 is Chris Morgan,
Number 2 is Chris Morgan,
Number 3 is Chris Morgan,
Number 4 is Chris Morgan,
Number 5 is Chris Morgan,
Number 6 is Chris Morgan...

We all dream of a team of Chris Morgans,
A team of Chris Morgans,
A team of Chris Morgans...

CHRIS MORGAN 2

One Chrissy Morgan,
There's only one Chrissy Morgan.
One Chrissy Morgan,
There's only one Chrissy Morgan,
One Chrissy Morgan.

CHRIS PORTER

If Porter scores, we're on the pitch,
If Porter scores, we're on the pitch,
If Porter scores, we're on the pitch,
If Porter scores, we're on the pitch...

CHRIS PORTER 2

Benteke is w*nk, Benteke is w*nk,
We've got Chris Porter,
Benteke is w*nk.

CHRIS WILDER

It was our 6th year in divison one when
Chris Wilder came home,
He's taking us right to top,
He is one of our own,
He is one of our own.

CHRIS WILDER 2

He's one of our own,
He's one of our own,
Chrissy Wilder,
He's one of our own...

CHRISSY WILDER AND ALAN KNILL

Chrissy Wilder and Alan Knill,
Chrissy Wilder and Alan Knill,
Chrissy Wilder and Alan Knill,
Chrissy Wilder and Alan Knill...

CHRISTIAN NADE

Ole ole ole Nade,
Ole ole ole Nade,
Ole ole ole Nade,
Ole ole ole Nade...

COLIN ADDISON

Here's to you Colin Addison,
We all hope that you will score a goal.

COLIN ADDISON 2

This is to you Colin Addison,
We all love you more than you will know,
Oh oh oh...

COLIN ADDISON 3

Addy Addy Addy Addy Addison
Addy Addy Addy Addy Addison...

COLIN ADDISON 4

He's here, he's there,
He's every f**king where,
Addison, Addison.

COLIN MORRIS

Ging Gang,
Colin Colin Colin Colin Morris on the wing,
On the wing.

COULDN'T SELL ALL YOUR TICKET

Sell all your tickets,
You couldn't sell all your tickets,
Sell all your tickets,
You couldn't sell all your tickets...

DANNY WILSON

There's only one Danny Wilson,
One Danny Wilson,
Used to be s**te, now he's alright,
Walking in a Wilson wonderland.

DAVE JONES

There's only one Dave Jones,
One Dave Jones,
With a packet of sweets, a Portuguese tan,
Dave Jones has got Madaliene McCann.

DAVID MCGOLDRICK

Oh David McGoldrick,
Oh David McGoldrick,
Oh David McGoldrick,
Oh David McGoldrick...

DAVID PLEAT

Cheer up David Pleat,
Oh what can it mean,
To a kerb crawling b**tard,
And a s*it football team.

DEAN HENDERSON

Deano, Deano, Deano, Deano...

DER DER DER DER SUFC

Der der der der der der der SUFC,
Der der der der der der der SUFC...

DINGLES WHAT'S THE SCORE

Dingles, what's the score,
Dingles Dingles what's the score?

DON'T YOU EVER

Don't you ever,
Don't you ever,
Lower your standards,
Supporting Sheffield Wednesday,
Be a Blade,
Be a Blade,
Sheffield Wednesday's nothing to be scared of.

DON'T TAKE ME HOME

Don't take me home,
Please don't take me home,
I just don't want to go to work,
I want to stay here,
Drink loads of beer,
Please don't, please don't take me home.

EASY

Easy, Easy, Easy, Easy, Easy, Easy...

EDDIE COLQUHOUN

Whenever you're sad,
Whenever you're blue,
Whenever your troubles are many,
To win the cup we'll fight like f*ck,
Just like Eddie,
Eddie Eddie Colquhoun.

EIGHTEEN EIGHTY NINE

No Pig fans in town,
No Hillsborough to sadden my eyes,
Jack Charlton is dead,
And the Pig fans have fled,
And the year is Eighteen Eighty Nine...

EMPTY SEATS

They're here,
They're there,
They're every f*cking where,
Empty seats,
Empty seats.

ENDA STEVENS

Enda,
Oh Enda Stevens goes down the wing for,
Sheffield United, Sheffield United...

ENGLAND'S NUMBER ONE

England's, England's number one,
England's number one...

ETHAN EBANKS-LANDELL

Last Christmas I gave you my heart,
But the very next day you gave it away,
This year, to save me from tears,
I gave it to Ebanks Landell.

EVERYWHERE WE GO

Everywhere we go,
Everywhere we go,
It's the Shoreham boys making all the nois
Everywhere we go.

FALLING IN LOVE WITH YOU

Take my hand,
Take my whole life too,
But I can't help,
Falling in love with you,
United, (clapping),
United, (clapping),
United, (clapping)...

FOLLOW FOLLOW FOLLOW

Follow Follow Follow,
Sheffield United's the team to follow,
We've got Sammon and Sharpey,
Che and McNulty,
And Diego Di Girolamo...

FOREVER AND EVER

Forever and ever,
We'll follow our team,
We're Sheff United,
We rule supreme,
We'll never be mastered,
By no Wednesday b*stards,
We'll keep the red flag, flying high...

GARY MADINE

Gary Madine the washing Machine,
Gary Madine the washing Machine,
Gary Madine the washing Machine.

GEORGE BEST

Georgie Best superstar,
Carries a handbag and wears a bra.

GET A PROPER JOB

Get a proper job,
Get a proper job,
Get a proper job,
Get a proper job...

GET YOUR T*TS OUT

Get your t*ts out, get your t*ts out,
Get your t*ts out for the lads,
Get your t*ts out for the lads...

GLORY GLORY SHEFFIELD UNITED

Glory, glory Sheff United,
Glory, glory Sheff United,
Glory, glory Sheff United,
And the Blades go marching on on on.

GOING DOWN GOING DOWN

Going down, going down, going down,
Going down, going down, going down,
Going down, going down, going down
Going down, going down...

GREASY CHIP BUTTY

You fill up my senses,
Like a gallon of Magnet,
Like a packet of woodbine,
Like a good pinch of snuff,
Like a night out in Sheffield,
Like a greasy chip butty,
My Sheffield United,
Come thrill me again,
Nah, nah, nah, nah, nah, nah, oooh,
Nah, nah, nah, nah, nah, nah, oooh...

HARK NOW HEAR

Hark now here United sing,
The Wednesday ran away,
And we will fight for ever more,
Because of Boxing Day...

HARRY HASLAM AND DANNY BERGARA

Harry Haslam, Danny Bergara bibbety
bobbity boo,
Put 'em together and what have you got?
Top of Division 2.

HEADS KICKED IN

You're going to get your f**king heads
kicked in,
You're going to get your f**king heads
kicked in...

HELLO HELLO

Hello, hello,
We are the Shoreham boys,
Hello, hello,
We are the Shoreham boys,
And if you are a Wednesday fan,
Surrender or you'll die,
Cos we all follow United...

HELLO HELLO 2

Hello, hello, Shoreham aggro,
Hello, hello, Shoreham aggro...

HE'S A BLADE

He's a Blade and he's a blade,
Na na na na,
He's a Blade and he's a blade,
Na na na na...

HODGY

Hodgy, Hodgy, buy us Mick Jones,
Hodgy, buy us Mick Jones.

HODGY IS BETTER THAN YASHIN

Aye, aye, aye, aye,
Hodgy is better than Yashin,
Mick Jones is better than Eusebio,
And Wednesday are in for a thrashin.

HOTPOT

You can shove your f*cking hotpot up your
a*se,
You can shove your f*cking hotpot up your
a*se,
You can shove your f*cking hotpot,
Shove your f*cking hotpot,
Shove your f*cking hotpot up your a*se...

HOWARD KENDALL

There's only one Howard Kendall,
One Howard Kendall,
Whiskey in hand,
A couple of cans,
Stumbling in a Kendall wonderland.

I DO

I do I do I do I do, I do, I love United,
We whistled and sang,
'Til Shoreham Street rang,
We'll win the cup and the league.

I DON'T KNOW WHY

The Rotherham (Substitute as necessary)
sing,
I don't know why,
But after the match, they're going to die.

I HEAR THE SOUND

I hear the sound of distant bums,
Over there, over there,
How do they smell,
(Clap, clap, clap, clap),
Like f**king hell.

I LIKE BEER AND CHEESE

I like beer and I like cheese,
And I like the smell of the westerly breeze,
But most of all I like to see,
Bare women (Clap, clap clap),
Bare women (Clap, clap clap).

I MET A WEDNESDAY FAN

One day I went a wandering,
Along the cliffs of Dover,
And there I met a Wednesday fan,
So I kicked the bar steward over.

I WANT TO GO HOME

I want to go home,
I wanna go home,
This place is a s**t hole,
And I wanna go home.

IAN PORTERFIELD

We'll take more care of you Porterfield
Porterfield...

IAN RUSH

Ian Rush,
He's got a f**kin big nose,
He's got a f**kin big nose,
He's got a f**kin big nose.

I'M A BOW LEGGED CHICKEN

I'm a bow legged chicken,
I'm a knock kneed hen,
Ain't had a wank since I don't know when,
I walk with a waddle and I talk with skwark,
Doing the Shoreham boot walk.

IN OUR SHEFFIELD HOME

In our Sheffield home,
We stand under a statue in Fitzalan Square
Speak in an accent exceedingly rare,
In our Sheffield home.

IN THE LIVERPOOL SLUMS

In the Liverpool slums,
You look in a dustbin for something to eat,
You find a dead rat and you think it's a treat
In the Liverpool slums...

IN THE LIVERPOOL SLUMS 2

In the Liverpool slums,
Your dads in the nick,
And your mums on the game,
You can't get a job 'cos your too f**king
thick.

IS THERE A FIRE DRILL

Is there a fire drill,
Is there a fire drill,
Is there a fire drill,
Is there a fire drill...

IS THIS A LIBRARY

Is this a Library,
Is this a Library,
Is this a Library,
Is this a Library...

IT'S ALL QUIET

It's all gone quiet over there,
All gone quiet over there,
All gone quiet,
All gone quiet,
It's all gone quiet over there.

JACK O'CONNELL

Oh Jack O'Connel's Magic,
He wears a magic hat,
And if you throw a brick at him,
He'll heads the f**ker back,
He'll head it to the left,
He'll head it to the right,
And when we win promotion,
We'll sing this song all night...

JACKIE CHARLTON

Jackie Charlton's f**ked it up again,
Jackie Charlton's f**ked it up again...

JAMIE MURPHY

Who needs Messi when you got Jamie
Murphy,
Who needs Messi when you got Jamie
Murphy,
Who needs Messi when you got Jamie
Murphy,
Oooh Jamie Murphy.

JAMIE WARD

Do war do Wardy do war day,
Do war do Wardy a a...

JAMIE WARD 2

He'll shoot,
He'll score,
He's only 5 ft 4",
Jamie Ward Jamie Ward.

JIMMY HAGAN

Wonderful, wonderful Jimmy Hagan...

JINGE BELLS

Jingle Bells, Jingle Bells,
Jingle all the way,
Oh what fun it is today,
United won away.

JOHN FLECK

Johnny Fleck drinks Irb-bru,
He is our Scottish hero, on a free from
Coventry,
He cost us f**kin zero,
Five foot four and hard as f**k,
He gets the Blades excited,
Shove your Wendesday up your a*se,
Cos we are Sheffield United.

JOHN MACPHAIL

John McPhail,
John McPhail,
John McPhail,
John McPhail...
(Whilst jumping up and down)

JOHN TUDOR

Tudor, Tudor, Tudor,
Score another goal for me,
Tudor, Tudor, Tudor,
We've seen him on TV,
We haven't had a goal since lunchtime,
And now it's half past three,
So Tudor Tudor Tudor,
Score another goal for me.

JOHN TUDOR 2

Ei, ei ei o,
Up the table we wil go,
When we win promotion,
This is what we'll sing,
We all love you, we all love you,
Tudor is the King.

JUMP UP TURN AROUND

Jump up turn around, kick him in the
b**locks,
Jump up turn around, kick him in the head
Jump up turn around, kick him in the
b**locks,
Jump up turn around, kick him in the head
Ohhh lordy kick him in the b**locks,
Ohhh lordy kick him in the head,
Ohhh lordy kick him in the b**locks,
Ohhh lordy kick him in the head...

KEEP BRAMALL LANE IN OUR HEARTS

Keep Bramall Lane in our hearts,
Keep us Blades,
Keep Bramall Lane in our hearts we
say,
Keep Bramall Lane in our hearts,
Keep us Blades,
Keep us Blades 'Til our dying day.

KEITH EDWARDS

Nobody puts the ball in the net like
Edwards,
Keith Edwards.

KEITH TREACY

Keith Treacy, Keith Treacy,
Running down the wing.
Keith Treacy, Keith Treacy,
Hear United sing,
Loved by the Reds,
Hated by the Blues,
Keith Treacy Keith Treacy Keith Treacy.

KEN MCNAUGHT

Ken McNaught, Ken McNaught,
The best payer the Blades ever bought,
He can score with his head,
He can score with his foot,
He's so good he can score with his nuts.

KEVIN BLACKWELL

S U F C Kevin Blackwell's Barmy army,
S U F C Kevin Blackwell's Barmy army.

KEVIN BLACKWELL 2

Blackwell, Blackwell knock him out,
Blackwell knock him out,
Blackwell, Blackwell knock him out,
Blackwell knock him out.

KIERON FREEMAN

Down the right, down the right,
Kieron Freeman is the white Cafu.

KIERON FREEMAN 2

Ain't nobody, like Kieron Freeman,
Makes me happy, makes me feel this way.

LANCASHIRE

Lancashire, w*nk, w*nk, w*nk,
Lancashire, w*nk, w*nk, w*nk,
Lancashire, w*nk, w*nk, w*nk,
Lancashire, w*nk, w*nk, w*nk...

LEE HENDRIE

Lee Hendrie s**gged your mum,
Lee Hendrie s**gged your mum,
And now your gonna believe us,
And now your gonna believe us,
Lee Hendrie s**gged your mum...

LEE STRAFFORD

Can we paint a stand for you,
When you can't afford paint,
And your grounds in a state,
Thank Lee Stafford...

...When you attendance is poor,
And he's screaming for more,
Thank Lee Stafford.

When the fudders are right,
And your bookkeeping's sh*te,
Thank Lee Stafford.

When your investment ain't here,
By the end of the year,
Thank Lee Stafford.

LEEDS ARE FALLING APART AGAIN

Leeds,
Leeds are falling apart again,
Leeds,
Leeds are falling apart again...

LEON CLARKE

Oh Leon Clarke is magic,
He wears a magic hat,
He could of stayed at Wednesday,
But no he said f**k that,
He passes with his left,
He passes with his right,
And once we've beat those f****ng pigs,
We'll sing this song all night.

LEON CLARKE 2

Leon's on fire, your defence is terrified,
Leon's on fire, your defence is terrified,
Leon's on fire, your defence is terrified,
Leon's on fire,
Ohhh na na na na na na na na na na na...

LET'S GO MENTAL

Let's go f*cking mental,
Let's go f*cking mental,
La la la-la,
La la la-la...

LYS MOUSSET

Ole ole ole,
Moussett Moussett...

MAKE US MIGHTIER YET

We've got Hope and Curric,
Gil Reece on the wing,
Derden in the centre,
And Hockey is the king.

Higher still and higher shall our bounds be
set,
Harris who made us mighty,
Make us mightier yet.

MARK TODD

Mark Todd,
Poor sod,
Where's your Barnet gone,
You've lost your hair,
But we don't care,
Blades are number one.

MARLON KING

Punches girls in the eye,
He got caught now he's doing time,
They bust his ring in "D" wing,
They're all bumming Marlon King.

MATCH OF THE DAY

Some talk of Bobby Charlton,
Some talk of Francis Lee,
Some talk of Dennis Law,
And Mike Summerbee,
But Tony is the greatest,
And Tony is the king,
With Dearden scoring goals,
And Alan Woodward on the wing...

MAULED BY THE TIGERS

Mauled by the Tigers,
You're getting mauled by the Tigers,
Mauled by the Tigers,
You're getting mauled by the Tigers...

MICHAEL BROWN

Number 1, is Michael Brown,
Number 2, is Michael Brown,
Number 3, is Michael Brown,
Number 4, is Michael Brown,
Number 5, is Michael Brown...

Number tennnnnnnn, is Brian Deane,
Number 11, is Michael Brown.

We all dream of a team of Michael Brown,
A team of Michael Brown,
A team of Michael Brown...

MICHEAL JONES

Micheal Jones, Michael Jones,
Is it true what mummy says,
You won't come back oh no, no.

MICK JONES

M-i,
M-i-c,
M-i-c-k,
Mick Jones.

MICK JONES 2

When your smiling, when your smiling,
The whole word smiles with you,
And when your laughing, when your
laughing,
The sun comes shining through...

...But when your crying,
You bring on the rain,
So stop your crying be happy again.

So when your smiling, when your smiling,
The - Whole - World - Smiles - With - You,
Na na na nana,
The - Whole - World - Smiles - With,
M-i,
M-i-c,
M-i-c-k,
Mick Jones.

MIND THE GAP

Mind the gap, mind the gap Sheffield
Wednesday,
Mind the gap, mind the gap we say,
Mind the gap, mind the gap Sheffield
Wednesday,
You f**king told us you were on your way...

MOLLY MALONE

In Sheffield's fair City,
Where the maids are so pretty,
There once was a maiden called Molly
Malone,
As she wheeled her wheel barrow,
Through the streets broad and narrow,
Singing (Clap, clap) The blades / United.

NATHAN BLAKE

He's black, he's mean,
He raids fruit machines,
And his name is Nathan Blake.

NEIL SHIPPERLEY

He's fat, he's round,
His a*se drags on the ground,
Shipperley, Shipperley.

NICK MONTGOMERY

His name is Nick,
(His name is Nick),
Montgomery,
(Montgomery),
His name is Nick Montgomery,
He's got a touch like a rapist,
His name is Nick Montgomery...

OH MANCHESTER

Oh Manchester, oh Manchester,
Is full of s*it, is full of s*it.

OLI MCBURNIE

He is a striker he's our number nine,
Scoring goals in the red and white,
Twenty million and he came from Swansea
And he goes by the name of Mcburnie.

ON ILKLA MOOR BAHT 'AT (YORKSHIRE DIALECT)

Wheear 'ast tha bin sin' ah saw thee, ah saw thee,
On Ilkla Mooar baht 'at,
Wheear 'ast tha bin sin' ah saw thee, ah saw thee,
Wheear 'ast tha bin sin' ah saw thee...

...On Ilkla Mooar baht' at,
On Ilkla Mooar baht' at,
On Ilkla Mooar baht' at,
Tha's been a cooartin' Mary Jane,
Tha's bahn' to catch thy deeath o' cowd,
Then us'll ha' to bury thee,
Then t'worms'll come an' eyt thee oop,
Then t'ducks'll come an' eyt up t'worms,
Then us'll go an' eyt up t'ducks,
Then us'll all ha' etten thee,
That's wheear we get us ooan back.

ON ILKLA MOOR BAHT' AT (STANDARD ENGLISH)

Where have you been since I saw you, I saw you,
On Ilkley Moor without a hat,
Where have you been since I saw you, I saw you,
Where have you been since I saw you...

...On Ilkley Moor without a hat,
On Ilkley Moor without a hat,
On Ilkley Moor without a hat,
You've been courting Mary Jane,
You're bound to catch your death of cold,
Then we will have to bury you,
Then the worms will come and eat you up,
Then the ducks will come and eat up the worms,
Then we will go and eat up the ducks,
Then we will all have eaten you,
That's where we get our own back.

ON THE MARCH WITH WILDER'S ARMY

We're on the march with Wilder's army,
We're not going to Wembley,
And we don't give a f*ck,
Cos the Blades are going up,
Cos United are the greatest football team..

PAUL COUTTS

1,2,3,4, oh ay oh,
Our centre mid is Couttsy, oh ay oh,
He was on free from Derby, oh ay oh,
He never gives the ball away...

PAUL DEVLIN

The spice girls are all s**ppers,
And posh, she cannot sing,
And when she's s**gging Beckham,
She thinks of Paul Devlin,
Paul Devliiiiin Paul Devliiiin.

PETER NDLOVU

Peter Ndlovu,
Peter Ndlovu,
Peter Ndlovu,
Peter Ndlovu...

QUE SERA SERA

Que sera sera,
Whatever will be, will be,
We're going to Wembley,
Que sera sera.

RICHARD STEARMAN

Do do do,
Stearman's f**king blindo.

ROLL ALONG SHEFFIELD UNITED

Roll along Sheffield United roll along,
Put the ball in the net where it belongs,
When Hagan gets the ball, it's sure to be a goal,
Roll along Sheffield United roll along.

RON ATKINSON

He's fat, he's round,
He's taking Wednesday down,
Atkinson Atkinson.

SACK THE BOARD

Sack the board, sack the board, sack the board,
Sack the board, sack the board, sack the board,
Sack the board, sack the board, sack the board,
Sack the board...

SACK THE PIG

Sack the pig, sack the pig, sack the pig,
Sack the pig, sack the pig, sack the pig,
Sack the pig, sack the pig, sack the pig,
Sack the pig...

SANDER BERGE

He's Norwegian,
He plays for the blades with John Egan,
We're playing in Europe next season,
With Sander Berge.

He's Norwegian,
With Norwood and Fleck he's the reason,
We're playing in Europe next season
With Sander Berge.

SCORING FOR FUN

We're scoring for fun,
We're scoring for fun,
We're Sheffield United,
We're scoring for fun...

S*IT GROUND NO FANS

S*it ground, no fans,
S*it ground, no fans,
S*it ground, no fans,
S*it ground, no fans...

SHALL WE SING A SONG FOR YOU

Shall we sing a,
Shall we sing a,
Shall we sing a song for you,
Shall we sing a song for you...

SHEFF UNITED

Sheff United,
Sheff United,
Sheff United...

SHEFFIELD IS WONDERFUL

Oh Sheffield,
(Oh Sheffield),
Is wonderful,
(Is wonderful),
Oh Sheffield is wonderful,
It's full of t**s f**ny and United,
Oh Sheffield is wonderful...

SHEFFIELD UNITED AT ROME

I'm a rambler,
I'm a rambler,
I'm a long way from home.
I will follow United from Sheffield to Rome
I will eat when I'm hungry,
I will drink when I'm dry,
I'm a rambler, I'm a rambler,
And a Blade till I die...

SHEFFIELD UNITED FC

S and a H,
And an E and an F,
F and a I E L D,
U N I,
T ED,
Sheffield United FC...

SHEFFIELD WEDNESDAY'S F**ED IT UP AGAIN

Sheffield Wednesday's f**ked it up again,
Sheffield Wednesday's f**ked it up again,
Sheffield Wednesday's f**ked it up again...

SHEFFIELD SHEFFIELD

Sheffield, Sheffield, Sheffield, Sheffield...

SHOES OFF

Shoes off if you hate Wednesday,
Shoes off if you hate Wednesday,
Shoes off if you hate Wednesday,
Shoes off if you hate Wednesday...

SHOREHAM

Shoreham's here,
Shoreham's there,
Shoreham's every f**king where,
Na na na, na na na, na na...

SHOREHAM BOYS WE ARE HERE

Shoreham boys we are here woahhh woah,
Shoreham boys we are here woahhh woah,
Shoreham boys we are here, sh*g your
women, drink your beer,
Woooooah...

SHOREHAM REPUBLICAN ARMY

Aye, aye aye aye,
Shoreham Republican Army,
(We're barmy),
Wherever we go,
We fear no foe,
Cos we are the SRA.

SHOREHAM STREET

I was walking down Shoreham Street,
Singing a song,
I met a Wednedayite walking along,
So I kicked him in the b**locks,
And I kicked him in the head,
Now that Wednesdayite is dead.

SING WHEN YOU'RE WINNING

Sing when you're winning,
You only sing when you're winning,
Sing when you're winning,
You only sing when you're winning...

SINGING AT THE LANE

Singing at the Lane,
We're singing at the Lane,
What a glorious feeling,
We're winning again,
Wilder is happy, and we're happy too,
We're laughing and singing at the Lane.

SIT DOWN SHUT UP

Sit down, shut up,
Sit down, shut up,
Sit down, shut up...

SKY TV

Sky TV, is f**king s*it,
Sky TV, is f**king s*it...

SO EASY

So f**king easy,
Oh this is so f**king easy,
So f**king easy,
Oh this is so f**king easy...

STAND UP IF YOU CAN'T SIT DOWN

Stand up if you can't sit down,
Stand up if you can't sit down,
Stand up if you can't sit down,
Stand up if you can't sit down...

STAND UP IF YOU HATE WEDNESDAY

Stand up if you hate Wednesday,
Stand up if you hate Wednesday,
Stand up if you hate Wednesday,
Stand up if you hate Wednesday...

STEPHEN QUINN

Oh Stephen Quinny you are the love of my life,
Oh Stephen Quinny I'd let you s**g my wife
Oh Stephen Quinny I want ginger hair too.

STUART PEARCE

Pierce lost us the world cup,
Pierce lost us the world cup...

SUFC WE HATE WEDNESDAY

Ali alli allioooo,
Alli alli allioooo,
SUFC we hate Wednesday...

SUN JIHAI

He'll shoot,
He'll score,
He'll eat your labrador,
Sun Jihai,
Sun Jihai...

SWINGING A PIG

I never felt more like swingin' a pig,
From Hyde Park Flats, to Wadsley Bridge,
United, you got me swingin a pig,
As you do, as you do, as you f**king well
should do...

TAKE YOUR TIME SHEFFIELD UNITED

Take your time take your time Sheffield
United,
Take your time take your time I say,
Take your time take your time Sheffield
United,
Playing football the Norwich way.

THAT'S WHY YOU'RE GOING DOWN

That's why you're going down,
That's why you're going down,
That's why you're going down,
That's why you're going down.

THE BLADES

Na na na nana nanana The Blades,
Na na na nana na nana na na The Blades.

THE BLADES (CLAP)

(Clap, clap, clap, clap, clap),
The Blades,
(Clap, clap, clap, clap, clap),
The Blades...

THE BLADES ARE GOING UP

The Blades are going up,
The Blades are going up,
And now you're gonna believe us,
And now you're gonna believe us,
And now you're gonna believe us,
The Blades are going up...

THE CITY IS OURS

The city is ours, the city is ours,
F**k off Wednesday,
The city is ours...

THE FAMOUS SHEFFIELD WEDNESDAY

The famous Sheffield Wednesday went
along to see the pope,
The famous Sheffield Wednesday went
along to see the pope,
The famous Sheffield Wednesday went
along to see the pope,
And this is what he said, "F**k Off"

THERE IS A CIRCUS IN THE TOWN

There is a circus in the town,
Jackie Charlton is the clown,
Roger Wylde an Tommy Tynan too,
They're the monkeys in the zoo.

THEY WON'T COME ON SHOREHAM

Their fans are all plastic and stands made of tin,
We'll drown all the b**tards in bottles of Gin,
Ten thousand wednesdayites dead on the floor,
They won't come on Shoreham Street Kop any more.

THOSE WERE THE DAYS

Those were the days my friends,
We took the Stretford End,
We took the Shed,
The North Bank Highbury,
We'd fight wherever we choose,
We'd fight and never lose,
We are the Blades, because we are the Blades.

TONY CURRIE

His eyes they shone like diamonds,
They call him the king of the land,
And there stood Tony Currie,
Stood there with the cup in his hands.

TONY CURRIE 2

Tony Currie walks on water...

TRACKSUITS FROM MATALAN

Tracksuits from Matalan,
Tracksuits from Matalan,
Tracksuits from Matalan,
Tracksuits from Matalan...

TREVOR HOCKEY

Singing aye aye Hockcy,
Hockey aye,
Singing aye aye Hockey,
Hockey aye,
Singing aye aye Hockey,
Aye aye Hockey,
Aye aye Hockey,
Hockey aye...

UGO EHIOGU

Ugo Ehiogu,
Ugo Ehiogu,
Ugo Ehiogu.

Ugo,
Ugo,
Ugo.

UNITED

United, United, United, United...

UNITED UP WEDNESDAY DOWN

United up, Wednesday down,
Hallelujah,
United up, Wednesday down,
Hallelujah.

WE ARE THE SHOREHAM BOYS

We've travelled far and wide,
London to Merseyside,
But there is only one place I wanna be,
And that is Shoreham Street,
Where it is magnifique,
Where Wednesdayites lay down at our feet
Na na naaa na naaa, na na naaa na naaa...

WE ARE BLADES

We are Blades, we are Blades,
Oh we are, we are Blades...

WE ARE BLADESMEN

We are Bladesmen, we are Bladesmen,
Super Bladesmen, from the Lane,
We are Bladesmen, super Bladesman,
We are Bladesmen, from the Lane...

WE ARE GOING UP

We are going up,
Sing we are going up,
We are going up,
Sing we are going up...

WE ARE GOING UP 2

We are going up,
I said we are going up,
We are going up,
I said we are going up...

WE ARE PREMIER LEAGUE

We are Premier League,
I said we are Premier League,
We are Premier League,
I said we are Premier League...

WE ARE STAYING UP

We are staying up,
Say we are staying up,
We are staying up,
Say we are staying up...

WE ARE THE SHEFFIELD UNITED

We are the Sheffield United,
We play in the red white and black,
And we are so proud,
We shout it out loud,
Division One we're coming back.

WE ARE TOP OF THE LEAGUE

We are top of the league,
Sing we are top of the league,
We are top of the league,
Sing we are top of the league.

WE CAN SEE YOU SNEAKING OUT

We can see you, we can see you,
We can see you sneaking out,
We can see you sneaking out...

WE FORGOT THAT YOU WERE HERE

We forgot that, we forgot that,
We forgot that you were here,
We forgot that you were here...

WE HATE WEDNESDAY

Oh we hate Wednesday,
We hate Wednesday, we hate Wednesday,
We hate Wednesday, we hate Wednesday,
We hate Wednesday,
We are the Wednesday haters.

WE LOVE TO SEE UNITED WIN AWAY

We love to see United win away,
We love to see United win away,
Blades win away,
Oh Blades win away.

WE LOVE UNITED

We love United we do,
We love United we do,
We love United we do,
Oh United we love you...

WE WHISTLED WE SANG

We whistled and we sang,
Til the Shoreham Street rang,
And we'll win the Cup and the League.

WEDNESDAY WEDNESDAY

Wednesday, Wednesday, the coppers are
after you,
Wednesday, Wednesday, I'll tell you what
they'll do,
They'll tie you up with up with wire inside a
Black Maria,
So ring your bell and pedal like hell on a
bicycle made for,
U-N-I-T-E-D, Uniteeeeed.

WE'LL DO WHAT WE WANT

We'll do what we want,
We'll do what we want,
We're Sheff United,
We do what we want...

WE'LL SEE YOU ALL OUTSIDE

We'll see you all outside,
We'll see you all outside,
We'll see you all,
We'll see you all outside...

WE'LL SIT WHERE WE WANT

We'll sit where we want,
We'll sit where we want,
We're Sheff United,
We'll sit where we want...

WE'RE ALL F**KING W**KERS AT THE LANE

We're all f**king w**kers at the lane...

WE'RE GOING TO WIN THE LEAGUE

We're going to win the league,
We're going to win the league,
And now you gonna believe us,
We're going to win the league.

WE'RE NOT SINGING ANYMORE

We're not singing,
We're not singing,
We're not singing anymore,
We're not singing anymore...

WE'RE SENDING 'EM DOWN

We're sending 'em down,
We're sending 'em doooowwwwn,
One week on Sunday,
We're sending 'em down.

WE'RE SENDING 'EM DOWN 2

We're sending 'em down,
We're sending 'em doooowwwwn,
Hillsborough's a sh*t hole,
We're sending 'em down.

WE'RE SHEFFIELD UNITED

We're Sheffield United,
Nice to meet you,
And now we're back in division 2,
We've been away for far too long,
And now we're back to sing our song.

WE'RE THE FAMOUS SHEFFIELD UNITED

Wemberlee, Wemberlee,
We're the famous Sheffield United,
And we're going to Wemberlee.

WE'RE THE RED AND WHITE ARMY

We're the red and white army
We're the red and white army
We're the red and white army
We're the red and white army
We're the red and white army.

WE'RE THE TEAM THAT RULE

You've heard of Man United,
You've heard of Liverpool,
You've heard of Sheffield United and we're
the team that rule,
United play great football United play it
right,
And if you want to disagree there's going to
be a fight.

WHAT A NIGHT

Late September on a Sunday night,
Duffy scored and they were f**king sh*te,
What a feeling,
What a night,
Oh what a night,
Oh what a night,
Oh what a night.

WHAT THE HELL WAS THAT

What the f**k,
What the f**k,
What the f**king hell was that,
What the f**king hell was that...

WHAT YOU GONNA DO

Wednesday, what you gonna do,
You're going down to division two,
You won't win a cup,
You won't win a shield,
Your next derby game's against the
Chesterfield.

Oh Wednesday what you gonna do,
You're going down to division two,
You can take your trumpet,
Take your drum,
Cos you're gonna play with the Barnsley
scum.

WHAT'S IT LIKE TO SH*G A SHEEP

What's it like, what's it like,
What's it like to sh*g a sheep,
What's it like to sh*g a sheep...

WHEN I WAS YOUNG

When I was young, I had no sense,
I wanted a ticket, for 50 pence,
The only team, that I could watch,
Were the piggy c***s,
And they ripped me off.

We all hate wednesday,
We all hate wednesday,
We all hate wednesday.

WHEN THE BLADES GO MARCHIN

Oh when the Blades (Oh when the Blades)
Go marching in (Go marching in),
Oh when the Blades go marching in,
We want to be in that number,
Oh when the Blades go marching in.

WHEN YOU'RE STROLLING

When you're strollling, just strolling,
By the light of the silvery moon,
I don't envy the rich in their automobile,
A motorbike is phoney,
I'd rather s*ag a pony,
When you're strolling.

WHENEVER UNITED ARE PLAYING

Whenever you're sad, whenever you're blue,
Whenever United are playing,
Beneath the Kop we'll fight like f**k,
To keep the red flag flying.

WHERE WERE YOU

Where were you, where were you,
Where were you at Bramall Lane,
Where were you at Bramall Lane...

WHERE'S YOUR CARAVAN

Where's your caravan,
Where's your caravan,
Where's your caravan,
Where's your caravan...

WHERE'S YOUR FATHER

Where's your father,
Where's your father,
Where' your father referee,
You aint got one,
You're a b**tard,
You're a b**tard referee.

WHERE'S YOUR FORESKIN GONE

Where's your foreskin gone,
Where's your foreskin gone...

WHO ARE YA

Who are ya,
Who are ya,
Who are ya,
Who are ya...

WHO'S THAT COPPER

Dixon, Dixon.
Who's that copper with the helmet on,
Dixon of Dock Green,
On the beat all day, on the wife all night,
Who's that copper with the helmet on,
Dixon of Dock Green.

WILLIAM FOULKE

He's fat, he's round,
He weighs 400 pound,
Fatty Foulkes, Fatty Foulkes.

WINGS OF A SPARROW

If I had the wings of a sparrow,
And I had the a*se of a crow,
I'd fly over Hillsbrough tomorrow,
And sh*t on the ba**ards below, below,
Sh*t on, sh*t on,
Sh*t on the ba**ards below, below.

WOULDN'T IT BE LOVELY

All you need is a shovel and a pick,
A hand grenade and a walking stick,
A Wednesday fan to boot and kick,
Wouldn't it be lovely...

YORKSHIRE

Yorkshire, Yorkshire, Yorkshire, Yorkshire...

YOU'RE GOING HOME IN A AMBULANCE

You're going home in a Yorkshire / Sheffield ambulance (Clap, clap clap clap clap).

YOU'LL BE RUNNING DOWN THE ROAD

You'll be running down the road when we come,
(When we come),
You'll be running down the road when we come,
(When we come)...

...you'll be running down the road running down the road,
Running down the road,
Running down the road when we come.

Singing Eye-yai-yippee-yippee-yai,
Singing Eye-yai-yippee-yippee-yai,
Singing Eye-yai-yippee,
Eye-yai-yippee,
Eye-yai-yippee-yippee-yai,
The Blades are here.

YOU'LL NEVER FILL YOUR STAND

Jog on... jog on,
No hope, for your plans,
And you'll never fill your ground,
You'll never fill your ground...

YOUR CITY IS RED

Your city is red,
Your city is red,
Just like Sheffield your city is red.

YOUR SUPPORT

Your support,
Your support,
Your support is f**king s*it,
Your support is f**king s*it...

YOU'RE NOT FIT TO REFERRE

You're not fit,
You're not fit,
You're not fit to referee,
You're not fit to referee.

YOU'RE NOT SINGING ANYMORE

You're not singing,
You're not singing,
You're not singing anymore,
You're not singing anymore.

YOU'RE NOT VERY GOOD

You're not very good,
You're not very good,
You're not very, you're not very,
You're not very good.

YOU'RE S*IT AND YOU KNOW YOU ARE

You're s*it, and you know you are,
You're s*it, and you know you are,
You're s*it, and you know you are,
You're s*it, and you know you are...

Printed in Great Britain
by Amazon